Everything You Need to Know About *The Prince*

About Charles River Editors

Charles River Editors was founded by Harvard and MIT alumni to provide superior editing and original writing services, with the expertise to create digital content for publishers across a vast range of subject matter. In addition to providing original digital content for third party publishers, Charles River Editors republishes civilization's greatest literary works, bringing them to a new generation via ebooks.

Visit charlesrivereditors.com for more information.

Introduction

Niccolò Machiavelli (1469 – 1527)

"He who becomes master of a city accustomed to freedom and does not destroy it, may expect to be destroyed by it." – Machiavelli, *The Prince*

Niccolò Machiavelli was born in Florence on May 3, 1469, as Florence was undergoing its transition into the Renaissance, guided by the Medicis. Machiavelli was a public servant during the Republic, losing his office when the Medicis returned to power. Despite that, Machiavelli dedicated *The Prince* to the ruling Medici of the time, leading some today to still speculate whether the book was a satire. Regardless, *The Prince* remains one of the most influential political philosophies of history, and Machiavelli himself will forever be associated for the "ends justify the means" philosophy that he wrote about and which even today is called Machiavellian.

The Prince was eventually published in 1532, though evidence exists that the manuscript was circulated before this point, which was deemed more polite than physical publication. 27 years later, in 1559, the text was, unsurprisingly, registered to the Index Librorum Prohibitorum (the Catholic Church's list of banned books) on the grounds of immorality.

The text can generally be divided into four parts. Chapters 1-11 outline the different types of principalities, and the benefits and drawbacks of each, to "discuss how such principalities are to be ruled and preserved" (II.1). Chapters 12-14 discussed military force, including how to amass and maintain an army. But it is Chapters 15-23 that make the book infamous. In these chapters Machiavelli discusses the importance (or unimportance) of morality, claiming, "it is necessary for a prince wishing to hold his own to know how to do wrong, and to make use of it or not according to necessity" (XV.2). Thus, the "ends" justify the "means."

The Prince is just as notorious today as it was nearly 500 years ago, and Machiavelli's political philosophy has never been more relevant. *Everything You Need to Know About The Prince* is the perfect resource for understanding Machiavelli's seminal treatise, explaining the historical context within which Machiavelli wrote it, its philosophy and historical examples, its major themes, and its influential and enduring legacy. With *The Prince* and its underlying themes as relevant as ever today, get caught up quickly with this resourceful guide.

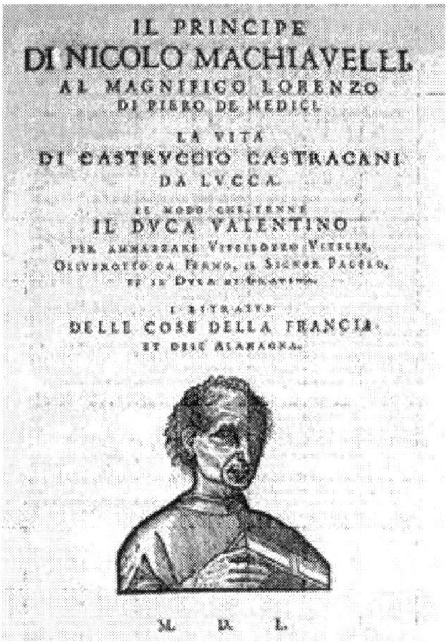
IL PRINCIPE
DI NICOLO MACHIAVELLI
AL MAGNIFICO LORENZO
DI PIERO DE MEDICI.
LA VITA
DI CASTRVCCIO CASTRACANI
DA LVCCA.
IL MODO CHE TENNE
IL DVCA VALENTINO
PER AMMAZZARE VITELLOZZO VITELLI,
OLIVEROTTO DA FERMO, IL SIGNOR PAVOLO,
ET IL DVCA DI GRAVINA.
I RITRATTI
DELLE COSE DELLA FRANCIA
ET DELL'ALAMAGNA.
M. D. L.

Early Title Page of *The Prince*

Historical Background

Niccolo Machiavelli was born in Florence, Italy on May 3, 1469. His father, Bernardo di Niccolò Machiavelli, was a noted lawyer and ensured that his son was well educated in grammar, rhetoric, and Latin. Machiavelli was apprenticed to a banker and eventually served on several Florentine councils. He was active in the political maneuverings of the province, including leadership of the city's militia. Machiavelli met with many important leaders of his day and was able to make erudite commentary on the state of Italy in his political treatise, *The Prince*.

Appreciating the scope of *The Prince* requires an understanding of Italy's social and political unrest during this time. During the fifteenth and sixteenth centuries, Italy was not the unified country we know today. The land was split into various city-states, each with its own political regime. In addition to the Papal States, the more significant areas covered in Machiavelli's text are Naples, Venice, Milan, and, of course, Florence. Each city-state had its own leader and was considered separate from the others. However, they were all Roman Catholic and under the sway of the papacy. The distinction between secular leadership and religious leadership was often blurred. However, the Pope's ability to excommunicate secular leaders gave him significant influence in public affairs outside of religion. As a result of this disarray, endless internal fighting occurred within each city-state, between the different city-states, and between the papacy and the city-states. Leaders rose and fell on a regular basis, and the land was far from stable.

Florence, in particular, has a rich history influenced by these insurrections. Prior to 1494, Florence was a hereditary principality ruled by the powerful Medici family. The excesses of the Church and government came under attack in Florence when **Girolamo Savonarola** (1452–1498) began preaching vehemently against the abuses of those in power. Savonarola and his followers, the Piagnoni, wanted to restructure the Florentine government into a republic which would be a "New Jerusalem."

Portrait of Savonarola

In 1494, the citizens of Florence followed Savonarola's advice and expelled the powerful Medici family. Instead of implementing a new principality, they established a republic. Savonarola was a strict leader of the new republic and caused much discontent amongst the people with his prophetic visions and austere laws. He was executed in 1498, and Piero Soderini (1450-1522) was named "Gonfaloniere for Life." Under Soderini's leadership, the Republic took Pisa and maintained a strong and steady presence in Italy. Florence prospered greatly by the more moderate leadership, which was aided by their Secretary of War, Niccolo Machiavelli.

This was also the period of time when Pope Alexander VI (1492-1503) held the papacy. Alexander (formerly Cardinal Rodrigo Borgia) and his son, Cesare Borgia, figure prominently in Machiavelli's text, and Borgia serves as both an example of strong leadership and of the difficulty of maintaining power when it is granted by a family member. But Alexander was not always popular as the Pope. In particular, Cardinal Giuliano della Rovere accused Alexander of simony—bribing members of the college of cardinals to get his papal seat. Della Rovere was not the only powerful Italian opposed to Alexander, so the Borgias needed help maintaining their power. Alexander saw this aid in the form of the French King Charles VIII, who wanted to conquer Naples (in South Italy). Alexander allowed the French army entry into Rome in exchange for his marital support. Charles agreed, and thus began a long and arduous relationship between Italy and France.

Pope Alexander VI

In 1503, Alexander died and his bitter rival, Cardinal della Rovere, became Pope Julius II (1503-1513). Julius first focused on uniting the city-states as much as possible. He brought together the two main Roman factions—the Orsinis and the Colonnas—which did much to stabilize Rome. He then turned his attention to foreign policy, befriending the king of France, the king of Spain, and the Holy Roman Emperor. He eventually overtook Venice and removed any remembrance of Alexander's sway there. Julius also established the Swiss Guard, the Pope's private army, ensuring he would not have to rely on mercenaries or the aid of others to fight his battles.

During this time, Machiavelli gained a unique position within the political climate. He travelled widely and personally met with Cesare Borgia, Julius II, King Charles of France, King Louis of France, and the Holy Roman Emperor Maximilian. He was well known by all of the major leaders and had a clear view to analyze the maneuverings, made apparent in *The Prince*.

However, by 1511, Julius was ready for the French to leave Italy. He formed the "Holy League," uniting Venice, Spain, the Holy Roman Empire, and England against the French. He also wanted Florence to support the Holy League, but Soderini declined in favor of the French.

At the Battle of Ravenna (1512), France's commander was killed, and the remaining soldiers returned home. The French officially left Italy, and Julius called a congress at Mantua, hoping to consolidate his power over the area. Because the Medici family had supported his anti-French campaign (and Soderini had not), Julius gave papal backing—and 6,000 Spanish troops—to Giovanni de Medici to retake Florence, which he did later that year.

As one of the pillars of the Florentine Republic, Machiavelli was an easy target for the Medicis, who wanted to show their strength by destroying those who opposed them. 1513 was an extremely bad year for Machiavelli. He was falsely accused of attempting to reinstate the Florentine Republic, and the Medicis arrested, imprisoned, and tortured him. He was eventually released later that year, but forced into house arrest in Persussina (South Florence). To add insult to injury, Giovanni de Medici was named Pope Leo X that same year, adding even more forces working against Machiavelli.

Pope Leo X

It seems uncanny to many scholars that 1513 was also the year Machiavelli wrote *The Prince*, with its lavish dedication to Lorenzo di Piero de Medici (Giovanni/Leo's nephew left in charge of Florence). Did Machiavelli hope the book would end his exile? Did he hope to make new alliances with the Medici family? Or was the book meant as a satire on the lack of morality in Italy's leadership? These questions are still debated.

Lorenzo de Medici

No one knows whether any of the Medicis ever saw a copy of the text, and Machiavelli was never released from exile, where he died on June 21, 1527. One must wonder how he felt about the ultimate sack of Rome (and the new Medici pope, Clement VII) by the Spanish just one month before his death.

The Prince was eventually published in 1532—Clement VII was still the pope. Evidence exists that the manuscript was circulated before this point, however, which was deemed more polite than physical publication. Twenty-seven years later, in 1559, the text was, unsurprisingly, registered to the Index Librorum Prohibitorum (the Catholic Church's list of banned books) on the grounds of immorality.

Clement VII

The Context of *The Prince*

Written in the Italian vernacular, rather than Latin, *The Prince* follows the basic format of "Mirror for Princes" genre, which includes Xenophon's *The Education of Cyrus*, Seneca's *De Clementia*, and Erasmus' *Education of a Christian Prince*. Allan Gilbert expands on the genre's influence in *Machiavelli's Prince and Its Forerunners* (1938), still considered one of the most thorough sources on inter-textuality. In this genre, the writer provides instruction for a newly appointed ruler, teaching him how best to use his power. Machiavelli was clearly aware of this genre, but whether he is adhering to it or satirizing it is still debatable.

The text can generally be divided into four parts. Chapters 1-11 outline the different types of principalities, and the benefits and drawbacks of each. The purpose of his text, Machiavelli claims is to "discuss how such principalities are to be ruled and preserved" (II.1). He fills these sections with historical examples of leaders who embodied good leadership, and those who didn't. Because of these historical references, this section can be hard for entry-level students to understand. Having a clear lecture before the reading or a heavily annotated text will prove useful.

The next section—sometimes included in the previous section—focuses on military force (Chapters 12-14). Machiavelli's service in the Florentine militia and as the Secretary of War influences this section, where he debates how to amass and maintain an army.

The third section of the treatise (Chapters 15-23) is the best recognized. Here, Machiavelli presents a radical view of relative morality, claiming, "it is necessary for a prince wishing to hold his own to know how to do wrong, and to make use of it or not according to necessity" (XV.2). A good leader will do anything possible to maintain his power because a healthy principality is founded upon stable leadership. Sometimes, maintaining a stable state means doing things that are considered immoral or sinful. However, this section assures leaders that the "ends" justify the "means." This section covers some of those possibilities.

The final section (Chapters 24-26) explains how and why Italy is in disarray—there is no strong leader. Everyone is so focused on fighting one another that the State suffers. That, in Machiavelli's view, will lead to a foreign power overtaking them (and, of course, he was right). He calls out to the people of Romagna, and to the Medicis in particular, to unite and strengthen Italy's potential power before it is too late.

Summary of Chapters 1-11

(Note on Citations: Since translations vary, all citations are given in chapter number, followed by paragraph number.)

Chapter One, "How Many Kinds of Principalities There Are, and by What Means They Are Acquired," is only one paragraph long. It essentially states that there are two forms of government: principalities and republics. He tells us that his book will deal only with principalities. This shouldn't come as a surprise, as Florence had shifted back to a principality only a year before the book's creation. Thus, the remaining chapters in this section break down the different types of principalities.

Chapter Two focuses on "Hereditary Principalities." Machiavelli presents the Duke of Ferrara as an example of a hereditary monarch who was able to withstand attacks because of his long-rooted heritage in Italy. A hereditary principality is always easier to maintain, because that is what the people are used to. However, Machiavelli also notes that a leader does not always need to rely on heritage for a stable principality.

As an important side note, it is useful to note that Lucrezia Bogia, Cesare Borgia's sister and Pope Alexander VI's daughter, was married to Alfonso D'Este, the Duke of Ferrara. His son, also the Duke of Ferrara, is the persona of Robert Browning's "My Last Duchess" [1842].

Alfonso D'Este, the Duke of Ferrara

Chapter Three is lengthier than the first two, focusing on "Mixed Principalities." By this, Machiavelli means leaders who conquer foreign lands—the principality is "mixed" since it includes both the original and new subjects of the prince. Machiavelli warns that mixed principalities work by a different set of rules. Oftentimes, people support a new ruler deposing a tyrant. They think their social situations will improve, and, for a time, they might. Eventually, however, things may turn out worse than before.

Machiavelli also warns new rulers that holding a conquered land can be difficult. He uses King Louis XII of France as an example. The king conquered Milan and made many powerful friends. But the king held his highest allegiance to the Pope (Alexander VI). On the surface, Louis did everything correctly: "he destroyed the minor powers, he increased the strength of one of the greater powers in Italy, he brought in a foreign power, he did not settle in the country, he did not send colonies" (III.16). But when he gave the spoils of war to the Pope, rather than the local nobles, Louis sealed his fate. The oppressed people revolted under the leadership of Duke Lodovico and ousted the French.

King Louis XII

A foreign ruler must learn from the French's fiasco. A prince who wishes to conquer a foreign principality must (1) know the language and customs and (2) live in the conquered land to establish his martial presence. If he cannot live in the principality, he must set up a colony with loyal magistrates, strong military presence, and everyday citizens.

Additionally, a foreign prince must deal with his neighboring principalities by either conquering them or befriending them. In the first case, the prince eliminates any threat to his power. In the latter, he must continually worry about his allies turning against him, so he can only befriend neighbors who have significantly less power than he does.

However, some princes successfully hold foreign lands, as addressed in **Chapter Four**. Here, Machiavelli discusses which foreign lands are easier to conquer and hold. He uses the French and the Turks as two opposing examples.

The Turks' system of government works by having one clear prince. There is no nobility; rather, the prince hires ministers and regents whose only power derives from the prince (that is, they have no wealth or power or land unless the prince gives it to them). On the other hand, the French government is based on both a prince and a complex system of powerful nobles. Because the nobles are hereditarily wealthy through landownership, they are less dependent on the prince. A conquering prince must take these differences into consideration when invading foreign lands.

Overthrowing a native prince of the Turks is difficult because his reagents have more to lose if they are conquered. But overthrowing a French prince is easier because the nobles don't lose any power during changes of leadership. This makes the nobles less likely to support their native king (if the conquering prince's forces are strong enough).

Gaining a foreign principality is quite different than maintaining leadership once there. While systems like the Turks' would be difficult to conquer, the foreign prince will have an easier time consolidating and maintaining his power once the fighting is done. The regents, "being all slaves and bondmen," do not have a unified power to revolt (IV.3). The noble barons of foreign lands based on a system like the French's, however, have considerable power, and they can unite to maneuver against the foreign prince, especially when he returns to his native lands. Each new foreign invasion must be waged differently, depending on the social contract of the society.

Chapter Five introduces the concept of the Oligarchy. At times, princes have conquered lands, but allowed the citizens to maintain their own laws and customs. The only change is the nominal change in the prince. If both the conquering and conquered lands have similar customs and laws (e.g. both are principalities, rather than one being a principality and one being a republic), an oligarchy is easier to incorporate. But Machiavelli ultimately contends that "he who becomes master of a city accustomed to freedom and does not destroy it, may expect to be destroyed by it" (V.2).

The topic of **Chapter Six** is principalities gained by ability, as opposed to those gained by heritage or gifting—note that the Medici rule over Florence was gifted by Julius II, rather than earned through fighting. Machiavelli mentions Moses, Cyrus, Romulus, and Theseus as successful leaders who have gained a principality by arms or ability. Gaining a principality through war is difficult; however, because they have proven their prowess and ascended by the support of the people, "Those who by valorous ways become princes, like these men, acquire a principality with difficulty, but they keep it with ease" (VI.5).

Chapter Seven looks to the recent past, rather than antiquity, for examples of principalities gained "either by the arms of others or by good fortune." Most anthologies reprint this section frequently, showing the progress of the Borgias and della Roveres (aka Alexander VI and Julius II). Machiavelli begins by asserting that men who easily rise by the people they are to govern have problems because they "stand simply upon the goodwill and the fortune of him who has elevated them—two most inconstant and unstable things" (VII.1).

Cesare Borgia serves as an example of how a prince can successfully maintain his power. Borgia's father, Alexander VI, gave leadership over the Papal States to his son. He was able to do this using the strategy of "divide and conquer": he caused a rift in the two major families who could oppose him, the Orsini and the Colonna. Alexander then allowed the French to march across Italy, as long as they supported Borgia's right to power. In all of these machinations, however, the Borgias made powerful enemies.

Cesare Borgia

Borgia's first job was to extinguish the powerful men who challenged his power. He gave titles and wealth to both the Orsini and Colonna followers, which swayed their allegiance towards him. This lessened the threat from these powerful families.

The petty fighting between lesser families also was a priority, but Borgia needed to keep the appearance of a peacemaker, not a tyrant (lest the citizens unite and revolt). To quell the insurrections, Borgia hired Ramiro d'Orco, a man known for his brutality and shamelessness. D'Orco performed his job well, and soon the people stopped fighting amongst themselves. However, as Borgia foresaw, they also united in their hatred of d'Orco and his bloody reign.

Borgia used this opportunity to gain the love of the people—he had d'Orco publicly assassinated. The people entirely forgot that Borgia had given d'Orco carte blanche to torment them. Once Borgia killed d'Orco, the people viewed Borgia as their savior and stood behind his claim to power. In this way, Borgia smartly divided and conquered his enemies, through the power of others. He avoided the epithet of "monster," instead becoming "savior" (even though he was the cause of the discontent in the first place).

With the support of his country behind him, Borgia needed to rid the foreign threat posed by the French (whom his father had invited into the land). Borgia no longer needed the French to protect his claim, and the foreigners had a powerful army that could turn against Borgia at any time. He used the native Italians (who originally hated Borgia) to oust the French, which sealed his power as prince.

Thus, Machiavelli presents Borgia as an example of a good prince, who knew how to maneuver to maintain power. Nevertheless, Alexander VI soon became sick and was followed by Julius II, who had no love for the Borgias. This new, powerful enemy, combined with Borgia's own failing health, "frustrated his designs" (VII.11). Borgia's premature death was the cause of his lost power, showing that "Fortune" typically trumps the best of plans.

Chapter Eight shifts the focus to principalities gained by "Wickedness." Machiavelli notes that these methods may insure success, but they will not gain "glory" for the usurper. Therefore, when "seizing a state, the usurper ought to examine closely into all those injuries which it is necessary for him to inflict, and to do them all at one stroke so as not to have to repeat them daily; and thus by not unsettling men he will be able to reassure them, and win them to himself by benefits" (VIII.7).

The two main examples in this section are Agathocles (361-289 BCE) and, closer to home, Oliverotto da Fermo (1475-1502). The Sicilian Agathocles rose to power, becoming the leader of Syracuse. One of his first acts of office was to call a meeting of the city's powerful citizens, where he murdered them all to ensure his power. In the second example, Oliverotto da Fermo, one of Cesare Borgia's hired men, killed his uncle and his men at a banquet in his uncle's honor, taking his place as ruler.

Rather than warning would-be rulers away from these immoral actions, Machiavelli suggests that the deception be quick and thorough. Otherwise, the people will view the prince as a tyrant and revolt.

Machiavelli presents the extreme opposite of a ruler who uses vile tactics to gain power in **Chapter Nine**, concerning civil principalities. In this type of state, a "leading citizen becomes the prince of his country, not by wickedness or any intolerable violence, but by the favour of his fellow citizens" (IX.1). This help can come from two sectors: the nobility or the general populace.

While this may seem a better solution than patricide, Machiavelli warns that maintaining a civil principality is difficult. The prince who relies on help from powerful nobles finds himself "with many around him who consider themselves his equals, and because of this he can neither rule nor manage them to his liking" (IX.2). The nobles will never willingly cede their power, so the prince will always have to negotiate. Gaining power by the by the assent of the populace will be better for the prince because he "finds himself alone, and has none around him, or few, who are not prepared to obey him" (IX.2).

Nevertheless, there is only one prince, and there are thousands of citizens. A newly appointed leader, even one who was appointed by the people, must always be on guard. He does not have powerful nobles to support him against insurrections, so he must rely on his own guile. It may be best, according to Machiavelli, for a prince to establish his own nobles in this situation. This will allow him "to make and unmake them daily, and to give or take away authority when it pleases him" (IX.3). In this way, the prince will maintain rule through both love and fear (discussed more thoroughly in Chapter 17).

Chapter Ten analyzes "The Way in Which the Strength of All Principalities Ought to be Measured." Machiavelli suggests that determining whether or not a prince has the power to maintain his principality on his own is the best way to gage strength. If the prince does have this ability, his principality is more secure than if he does not.

However, princes without enough resources to support his land are not without recourse. Such leaders should follow the example of the Germans, who fortify their lands with strong defenses. In this way, the people are able to remain within the area without need for hiring mercenary soldiers. The main concern, then, would be any lands that fall outside of the defenses. Those lands can be burned and attacked, and the owners inside the fortifications can turn against the prince for his failure to defend their property.

Indeed, throughout the text, "property" and "women" are listed as the two main reasons that people revolt. Machiavelli claims that you can take a man's life, his father's life, or his son's life. But once a prince takes a man's property or his women, a revolt is inevitable.

Chapter Eleven provides the final type of principality: the ecclesiastical principality. Machiavelli argues that the ecclesiastical principality has the added benefit of religion to support the prince's power. Because "they are sustained by the ordinances of religion, which are so all-powerful," they "may be held no matter how their princes behave and live" (XI.1). He cites Popes Alexander VI and Julius II as two powerful princes who were able to aggrandize the church's power based on this premise. Of course, this offers little help for the secular ruler.

Summary of Chapters 12-14

Chapter Twelve addresses the topic of mercenary soldiers, something that Machiavelli opposed during his tenure in Florence. Because power shifted so quickly amongst the Italian city-states, new princes had little time to establish strong martial forces. Mercenary soldiers helped princes gain power and maintain authority. Although the "chief foundations of all states, new as well as old or composite, are good laws and good arms"(XII.1), a military is necessary as a back-up against internal insurrection or foreign invasion. However, mercenary soldiers have no loyalty and will switch allegiance for the right price. The Papal States, for example, had to hire mercenaries in the past (before Julius II established the Swiss Guard). Those mercenaries caused more problems for Italy than they have solved.

It's worth noting that Machiavelli staunchly opposed mercenaries in Florence, well before he wrote *The Prince*. He was instrumental in forming and leading the local militia, replacing the

Republic's use of mercenaries. This was one of his qualifications that led to his appointment as Florence's Secretary of War.

In addition to mercenaries, forming a new principality can often lead to auxiliaries and mixed soldiery, the topic of **Chapter Thirteen**. Auxiliaries are borrowed troops, used when a prince gets aid from a neighbor or ally. (A mixed soldiery, obviously, is made up of local soldiers and either auxiliaries and/or mercenaries.) According to Machiavelli, auxiliaries "are much more hazardous than mercenaries, because with them the ruin is ready made; they are all united, all yield obedience to others" (XIII.5). This creates a lose-lose situation for the prince. Firstly, the auxiliaries may not be powerful enough, and the prince loses his power. On the other hand, the auxiliaries may help the prince to gain or maintain his power; but then he is beholden to outsiders for their aid. Further, they may never leave, leaving foreign presence in the principality.

France's Louis XII exemplifies this hazard. Louis "abolished the infantry and began to enlist the Switzers" (XIII.9). This caused France's reputation as a strong martial force to diminish: "having raised the reputation of the Switzers, he has entirely diminished the value of his own arms, for he has destroyed the infantry altogether; and his men-at-arms he has subordinated to others, for, being as they are so accustomed to fight along with Switzers, it does not appear that they can now conquer without them" (XIII.9).

Chapter Fourteen addresses the prince's own involvement in martial rule. Instead of remaining safely in his fortress and relying on others to run his armies, "A prince ought to have no other aim or thought, nor select anything else for his study, than war and its rules and discipline" (XIV.1). To maintain his power, a prince must be a warrior; he must learn his lands and know how to plan attacks and defenses in all areas; he must communicate with his soldiers and advisors; and he must read about the best leaders history has to offer. Only by following this advice will a prince safely maintain his rule. "A wise prince ought to observe some such rules, and never in peaceful times stand idle, but increase his resources with industry in such a way that they may be available to him in adversity, so that if fortune changes it may find him prepared to resist her blows" (XIV.4).

Summary of Chapters 15-23

This section comprises the most controversial section of *The Prince*. In it Machiavelli presents the concept of relative morality (although he does not use that term). Instead of always adhering to a universal concept of right and wrong, Machiavelli presents a more "realistic" view of leadership.

Machiavelli explains in **Chapter Fifteen** that "every one will confess that it would be most praiseworthy in a prince to exhibit all the above qualities that are considered good; but because they can neither be entirely possessed nor observed, for human conditions do not permit it, it is necessary for him to be sufficiently prudent that he may know how to avoid the reproach of those vices which would lose him his state" (XV.2). This is one of the major areas where Machiavelli diverges from other political treatises. Prior to *The Prince*, treatises based their advice on a utopian foundation and advised their reader to act based on that presumption. Machiavelli, however, acknowledges that the world is not a perfect place and counsels his readers on the need to interpret each issue on its own merits and problems.

At the same time, a prince also needs to avoid the appellation of "tyrant," so "he need not make himself uneasy at incurring a reproach for those vices without which the state can only be saved with difficulty, for if everything is considered carefully, it will be found that something which looks like virtue, if followed, would be his ruin; whilst something else, which looks like vice, yet followed brings him security and prosperity" (XV.2). Every action a prince makes must be made to secure his power. A stable leadership is the only thing that will lead to the land's prosperity. If he must lie, or cheat, or steal, or murder, he is allowed to do so as long as the action is performed to promote his leadership and the principality's permanence.

Chapter Sixteen focuses on "Liberality and Meanness." According to a universal standard of morality based in Christian theology, liberality is always the moral action and meanness is always the immoral action. This precept does not always apply in real life, however. This is especially true with leaders. An overly generous prince can hurt his principality; by spending or giving freely, the prince may bankrupt his country. This would force him to regain the funds by heavy taxation. And, of course, no one likes high taxes, so the prince risks a revolt by the citizens.

Therefore, a good prince should not fear having a reputation for meanness, "provided that he has not to rob his subjects, that he can defend himself, that he does not become poor and abject, that he is not forced to become rapacious … for it is one of those vices which will enable him to govern" (XVI.3). Conversely, Pope Julius II had the reputation of being a liberal leader. However, he actually spent vast amounts of money, but the money was used to better the state and he never relied on taxation for the expenses. Therefore, there is no hard and fast rule. Sometimes liberality is a good thing; sometimes meanness is a good thing. Thus, an accurate analysis of the situation is key to knowing which way to govern.

Pope Julius II

Machiavelli does make one universal rule in this section: if a prince gains wealth from conquering other lands, he must always be liberal in rewarding his soldiers and supporters. This is the only way to secure future martial fame and expand the principality's power. Cyrus, Caesar, and Alexander comprise three examples of leaders who served their soldiers' will through this liberality and gained much power by doing so.

Caesar

Cruelty and Clemency are the topics of **Chapter Seventeen**. Again, clemency is a worthy attribute, while cruelty is held in contempt by a Christian morality, but Machiavelli suggests that both are needed in the case of new princes. The ruler must inspire enough fear in his subjects to avoid rebellion, but not enough to incite one.

This leads to Machiavelli's most cited paradoxes: whether it is better for a leader to be loved or feared. Simply put, "It may be answered that one should wish to be both, but, because it is difficult to unite them in one person, is much safer to be feared than loved, when, of the two, either must be dispensed with" (XVII.3). However, the prince must avoid being hated (especially by taking away his citizens' goods or women).

He provides many examples, but returns to Borgia: he was a cruel man, and had the reputation for cruelty, but "his cruelty reconciled the Romagna, unified it, and restored it to peace and loyalty" (XVII.1).

Machiavelli also references Hannibal and Scipio in this section. Although Scipio ultimately defeated Hannibal, Machiavelli attributes this to Fortune (discussed in more detail in Chapter 25), rather than the inherent leadership qualities in the pair. In fact, Hannibal is the more praiseworthy leader according to Machiavelli's interpretation. His "inhumane cruelty" and "boundless valor" allowed him to travel far and wide amassing land and power (XVII.5). Scipio, on the other hand, was a weak ruler whose soldiers were apt to dissention, and Machiavelli argues that Scipio was only effective within the bounds of a republic such as the one Rome had during the Punic Wars.

The line between love and fear is thin. In the end, men are fickle. If a prince bases his power on the people's love, he can quickly lose it when their tide of emotions changes. However, the prince who bases his power on the peoples' awe and fear has more control over his own destiny.

Chapter Eighteen is entitled "Concerning the Way in Which Princes Should Keep Faith." Machiavelli's view shouldn't come as a surprise to anyone in the modern world: a good leader must sometimes lie. For example, "a wise lord cannot, nor ought he to, keep faith when such observance may be turned against him, and when the reasons that caused him to pledge it exist no longer" (XVIII.1). However, a prince needs to avoid having a reputation for lying and vow-breaking, as he can lose allies and followers. Thus, he must create an external persona that projects one thing, even though his actions make go against that creation.

> [Y]ou have to understand this, that a prince, especially a new one, cannot observe all those things for which men are esteemed, being often forced, in order to maintain the state, to act contrary to faith, friendship, humanity, and religion. Therefore it is necessary for him to have a mind ready to turn itself accordingly as the winds and variations of fortune force it, yet, as I have said above, not to

diverge from the good if he can avoid doing so, but, if compelled, then to know how to set about it. (XVIII.4)

It becomes obvious, here, why the Catholic Church banned the book on the grounds of immorality.

While a prince must sometimes go against moral right, **Chapter Nineteen** stresses that he must also "Avoid Being Despised and Hated." In general, all rulers can be attacked on two levels—attack from within (his people) or attack from without (foreigners). The second is easier to avoid, surprisingly, because a strong army and reputation as a fearsome warrior will stave off future wars. But the first—the threat of internal insurrection—is even more troublesome for a new prince. Only by avoiding his people's hatred can a prince maintain his position.

Every prince will meet with people in his own faction that want to take his power. But these conspirators will only act if they have the support of the people. A rival lord can't just murder the prince in order to gain power (in "polite" societies); instead he will be labeled a traitor and killed, and another will take the place of the prince. This obviously does the conspirator little good. However, if the conspirator has the public's backing, he can displace the current prince. Therefore, maintaining a good reputation is paramount for any prince, especially new princes. Although he may have to perform unpopular actions, he must know where the boundaries lie. And he should be able to "spin" his actions to the public if he must act in an immoral manner.

Once again, Machiavelli does not provide a simple answer for how to complete this obstacle. He references several leaders, each with differing levels of cruelty and kindness. In the end, he suggests that a prince's actions should be based on the cultural needs of the moment, rather than a universal sense of right and wrong.

If a new prince has to be wary of internal revolt, should he arm his subjects? In **Chapter Twenty**, Machiavelli says, "yes." While this may seem counterintuitive, Machiavelli argues that princes who arm their subjects show that they trust their citizens. A more effective filial relationship strengthens the bond between ruler and subject, and the subjects then become more likely to use their weapons to fight *for* the prince, rather than against him.

Machiavelli also suggests that new princes should carefully assess their alliances, as many "have found more fidelity and assistance in those men who in the beginning of their rule were distrusted than among those who in the beginning were trusted" (XX.5). Scholars have read this section, in particular, as a direct appeal from Machiavelli to the Medici leadership. Although Machiavelli was originally against the shift from the Republic to the principality, this interpretation suggests Machiavelli is telling the Medicis he can still be a valuable asset to the new regime.

This Chapter further presents the topic of building fortresses in foreign lands to ensure the citizens' compliance. While fortresses are not inherently negative, a good prince should rely on his character rather than walls to maintain his power.

"Nothing makes a prince so much esteemed as great enterprises and setting a fine example," Machiavelli states in the opening to **Chapter Twenty-One** (XXI.1). Martial prowess is the main way a leader can complete this requirement. And Spain's King Ferdinand stands as Machiavelli's paragon of a leader who sets a good example for his people. Ferdinand expanded his lands, quelled discontent amongst his barons, and removed the Moors from Spain, "always using religion as a plea, so as to undertake greater schemes" (XXI.1). Here, Machiavelli unknowingly foretells Italy's own future submission to the Spanish in 1527.

King Ferdinand

A prince should always take a firm stance on any issue. He should be "either a true friend or a downright enemy" (XXI.3). When two foreign parties are fighting, a good prince will declare his position decisively. If he remains neutral, he will be distrusted by both factions and possibly destroyed, regardless of the winner. However, if he takes a position, he stands a better chance of maintaining his power, again regardless of the winner.

For example, if the prince fights valiantly and the side he supports wins, he will be rewarded for his efforts. If he fights valiantly and his side loses, the other king will recognize his prowess and seek an alliance with the prince, rather than risk fighting him. (Or, in Machiavelli's case, they might be imprisoned, tortured, and exiled…)

Three other acts are important for a prince to engage in. First, he should always support his subjects in their callings, as this will provide a stable economy. Second, he should provide festivals and other entertainments for the citizens to keep them diverted and amused. Finally, a prince should interact with his citizens, though he should likewise maintain an aura of awe.

A prince must also choose his secretaries and advisors carefully, as set out in **Chapter Twenty-Two**. Because the secretaries are seen as extensions of the prince, their actions will reflect on his ability to rule well. If he chooses them wisely, he will be considered wise. If he chooses them unwisely, he will be considered unwise. In general, all servants of the prince should have the best interest of the principality in mind, for "he who has the state of another in his hands ought never to think of himself, but always of his prince, and never pay any attention to matters in which the prince is not concerned" (XXII.3).

Once a prince employs a trustworthy servant, the prince must reward him for his good actions. However, the prince should also avoid being too lavish in his praise or dependence on his advisors. Doing so will keep the employees from growing overly forward and challenging the prince for power.

Chapter Twenty-Three focuses on flatterers and dissemblers amongst a prince's retinue. As Machiavelli previously discussed, a good prince will listen to the advice of his people, especially those closest to him that have knowledge on the issue. The prince should allow those advisors to speak freely and liberally, even if they oppose the prince's wishes. This leads to the benefit of the principality. Having only flatterers will not produce the same progress.

However, the prince must limit his citizens' freedom of open aversion to his wishes, as this may spread dissention. "Therefore a wise prince ought to hold a third course by choosing the wise men in his state, and giving to them only the liberty of speaking the truth to him, and then only of those things of which he inquires, and of none others; but he ought to question them upon everything, and listen to their opinions, and afterwards form his own conclusions" (XXIII.2).

Although history offers many examples of monarchs who rely on toadeaters and take bad advice, Machiavelli makes a bold move by offering the current Holy Roman Emperor Maximilian I (1486-1519) as an example of a leader who does not use his council wisely.

Summary of Chapters 24-26

The final section of *The Prince* switches from theoretical discussions to the current affairs of Italy at large, and Florence in particular. According to **Chapter Twenty-Four**, "the Princes of Italy Have Lost Their States," and the land is in disarray. Italy is ready for a new prince, and this prince can be a new prince rather than a hereditary one, especially as the older rulers have grown lazy and mismanaged their affairs. Only with a new prince can Romagna reach its true potential.

But Machiavelli warns that the new prince should not rely on fortune to place him in a position of power in **Chapter Twenty-Five**. He compares "Fortune" to a raging river,

> which when in flood overflows the plains, sweeping away trees and buildings, bearing away the soil from place to place; everything flies before it, all yield to its violence, without being able in any way to withstand it; and yet, though its nature be such, it does not follow therefore that men, when the weather becomes fair, shall not make provision, both with defences [sic] and barriers, in such a manner that, rising again, the waters may pass away by canal, and their force be neither so unrestrained nor so dangerous. (XXV.2)

Unlike France, Spain, and Germany, Italy does not have the barriers necessary to protect it from a flood. Because Fortune changes on a whim, a successful prince will understand the "spirit of the times" (XXV.4) and change accordingly. The best rulers evolve and adapt with changes, rather than staunchly oppose those changes. A good prince, then, is a risk-taker.

The Prince's final chapter, **Chapter Twenty-Six**, is "An Exhortation to Liberate Italy from Barbarians." The country needs a strong ruler, and "Italy, left as without life, waits for him who shall yet heal her wounds and put an end to the ravaging and plundering of Lombardy, to the swindling and taxing of the kingdom and of Tuscany, and cleanse those sores that for long have festered" (XXVI.3). Judging from the treatise's preface, Lorenzo de Medici and Pope Leo X are the best men for the job. Machiavelli tells them to learn from the Borgias' reign to expand Italy's greatness and prepare for any future hazards.

Major Themes

Universal vs. Relative Morality

Imagine that you walk into your home after work to find your spouse and children tied up and held at gunpoint by a serial killer. You, coincidentally, have a gun and an opportunity to shoot the man without harming your family. What is the moral action to take here?

According to the paradigm of universal morality, it is immoral to kill the man to save your family. It is better to sacrifice your child and even your own life to avoid sinning (and, according to Christian doctrine, God will reward you in the end). But according to the paradigm of relative morality, the moral action may be to kill the man and save the others. The end result will be better for you, and also the world at large. Students familiar with Utilitarianism will find this concept recognizable, although there are significant differences between the nineteenth-century movement and Machiavelli's text.

One of the reasons that *The Prince* was placed on the Catholic Church's banned books list was because it did not follow the Church's teaching of **universal morality**. The concept of universal morality states that certain actions are *always* right, and certain actions are *always* wrong. Lying, cheating, stealing, killing, and amassing wealth are always wrong according to Church doctrine. Charity, clemency, forgiveness, and honesty are always right according to Church doctrine.

Prior "mirrors for princes" adhere to the concept of universal morality—even the ancient texts that did not employ Catholicism as its basis had similar notions of right and wrong. The genre assumed that, if a leader embodies everything that is pure and good and just, his followers will learn by his example. Conversely, if a leader is manipulative and deceitful, his citizens will follow his example. Therefore, a leader should be universally moral, always doing the right thing, as that will lead to peace and harmony in the state.

But *The Prince* offers a different view. If a prince is always generous, he will lose all his money. If he is always clement, he will be taken advantage of. If he is always honest, he will be manipulated and cheated. Because of this, a prince cannot (and should not) follow universal precepts of morality. Instead, he should employ **relative morality**.

The concept of relative morality states that the moral action is determined by the situation, not a universal or God-given law. For example, Machiavelli states that it is right for a prince to break an oath "when the reasons that caused him to pledge it exist no longer" (XVIII.1). If a prince has formed a treaty with another country, saying that neither will enter the other's land with armed forces, and the other country enters the prince's lands with armed troops, should the prince keep his oath (the universally moral action) or break his oath and retaliate by sacking the other country as well? *The Prince* suggests that the "right" action should be determined by the situation at hand, rather than overarching theories.

The pejorative term "Machiavellian" refers to "the employment of cunning and duplicity in statecraft or in general conduct". The term, however, is an oversimplification of the statesman's argument and a bit of a misnomer. Machiavelli never suggests that a prince should completely disrupt the universal dichotomy of right and wrong. He merely presents situations where a prince who wants to act in the best interest of his people must weigh each situation as a separate entity. The text may be better seen as amoral, rather than immoral.

Realism vs. Idealism

Machiavelli writes,

> it being my intention to write a thing which shall be useful to him who apprehends it, it appears to me more appropriate to follow up the real truth of a matter than the imagination of it; for many have pictured republics and principalities which in fact have never been known or seen, because how one lives is so far distant from how one ought to live, that he who neglects what is done for what ought to be done, sooner effects his ruin than his preservation; for a man who wishes to act entirely up to his

professions of virtue soon meets with what destroys him among so much that is evil. (XV.1)

As mentioned, most "mirrors of princes" established a utopian ideal of leadership. A moral leader, always acting according to universal precepts, would make the world a moral place, while an immoral leader would imprint the world with his negative example. But, as most people would agree, the world is not a utopia. There are always people ready to kill, steal, and cheat. The always-virtuous leader will find himself deposed and his state in disarray.

Instead, sometimes people must perform immoral actions to bring about good. Before acting, a prince must determine whether the means justify the end. The sole purpose of a prince is to protect his realm and the livelihood of his people. He seeks to maintain his power not because he is power-hungry or mega-maniacal; he seeks to maintain his power because stable leadership provides the base for a stable state, which is good for everyone. In the early sixteenth century, Italy was not unified, and the land was open to internal and external threats. Because of this, the people suffered. According to Machiavelli, only a strong, unified leadership could heal the country's wounds. But in order to gain and maintain power, the leader would have to understand the realities of the world, rather than a utopian ideal.

In a utopian world, war would be unnecessary. Princes would settle disputes with rational negotiations.

Fortune vs. Free Will

According to ancient Greek and Roman philosophy, Fate governs human life (and even the gods). Everything is subject to this force and it is futile to struggle against it. Think, for example, of the Greek tragedies such as *Oedipus Rex*—the more Oedipus runs from the oracle's prophecy, the more he runs directly towards his fate. Medieval and Renaissance philosophers generally held to this ideal, but within a Christian framework (e.g. divine providence).

In Chapter Twenty-Five, Machiavelli does claim that humans are often subject to changes in Fortune: leaders rise and fall without rational cause. Nevertheless, fortune only governs half of mankind's actions; free will governs the other half. There are several actions that a good prince can take to avoid falling from power during changes in fortune: (1) he can prepare for the unexpected by always planning, even in seemingly prosperous times, (2) he can learn to adapt to new times and new modes of thought by remaining flexible, and (3) he can fight against the tide of fortune. It is this third point that sets his work apart from previous writers.

As his famous quote goes, "fortune is a woman, and if you wish to keep her under it is necessary to beat and ill-use her; and it is seen that she allows herself to be mastered by the adventurous rather than by those who go to work more coldly. She is, therefore, always, woman-like, a lover of young men, because they are less cautious, more violent, and with more audacity command her" (XXV.8). With enough desire and preparation, humans have the power to overcome any external forces.

Virtù vs. Virtue

While Machiavelli diverges from classical thought in terms of fate, his conception of virtuc is more classical than modern. In any translation, certain textual and linguistic nuances are overlooked or un-translatable. Machiavelli's use of the term "virtù" proves complicated for modern readers.

The Italian "virtù" typically translates to the English "virtue", but the denotation of the term is quite different. "Virtue" is traditionally associated with the universal set of Christian morals. Thus the leader with "virtue" follows the precepts of universal morality. The leader with "virtù," however, relies on an older, classical version of virtue. "Virtù" consists of the qualities necessary to be a good leader, but those qualities are culturally constructed and historically grounded (according to a relativist perspective). As a general example, some cultures view suicide as a positive action associated with the brave, while others consider it a grave sin associated with cowards.

Thus, Machiavelli's ideal "virtù" vastly differs from a twenty-first century construction of "virtue." Actions that the Renaissance Church saw as immoral (such as deception and murder) may actually be virtuous when read in this context.

Humanism

The Renaissance focused on the philosophy of humanism, which said that man and society were appropriate topics of study. Renaissance humanism, however, should not be confused with modern humanism, which is a more secular movement. Renaissance humanists still believed in the supremacy and omnipotence of God; they were (for the most part) Christians. But their ideas about free will and human nature were not incompatible with Christian teaching. Leo X (from the Medici family) is remembered as a humanist pope who focused on collecting and applying classical ideas of philosophy, art, and literature.

In humanism, morality and rationality form the basis of decision making, rather than direct revelation of God and tradition. *The Prince* is considered a humanist text because it relies on classical traditions, but also because it focuses on man. For example, the idea that man can struggle against fortune or fate (and win) is based on humanist principles. Additionally, Machiavelli is not concerned with the afterlife or the religious effects of princes' actions, merely their worldly manifestations and benefits.

Social Commentary vs. Social Satire

"The book is, first and foremost, a satire, so that many of the things we find in it which are morally absurd, specious, and contradictory, are there quite deliberately in order to ridicule ... the very notion of tyrannical rule." – Ian Johnston

Just how far should we take the precepts set forth in *The Prince* in earnest? Did Machiavelli really want princes to act according to his discourse, or did he mean the text to be a satire or expose of the tyrannical and immoral actions of leaders? Was it written to juxtapose republics and monarchies in such a way as to make clear the benefits of free republics over tyrannical monarchies? Authorial intention, of course, can never be wholly established (and some debate whether intent has anything to do with interpretation at all), but scholars still debate how we should read the text.

Machiavelli's relationship with the Medicis was not ideal. He was part of the Republic that originally ousted the family from Florence and fought against their restoration in 1512. The Medicis tortured, imprisoned, and exiled him from his hometown. So why would he want to lend support and knowledge to them?

Those who take the book at face value argue that Machiavelli wanted to ingratiate himself with the Medicis so he could return home. Parts of his text promote this view. In Chapter Twenty-One, for example, Machiavelli states that a good leader clearly takes a side during a battle. Even if he is on the losing side, the winner will recognize his prowess and seek an alliance with him. This can be read as an attempt to show the Medicis that, although he fought for the opposing side, he can still be a powerful ally despite the regime change.

Additionally, in Chapter Twenty-Three, Machiavelli notes that sometimes the best advisors are ones that originally opposed the prince. They can offer different perspectives on issues that flatterers cannot (or will not for fear of losing their place at court). This can be interpreted as Machiavelli's attempt to show how he could be one of those trustworthy advisors although he originally opposed the Medici rule.

The use of the Borgias as the cornerstone of effective leadership may seem odd. Why wouldn't Machiavelli have used Medici rulers instead? The answer is simple: the Borgias blended religious leadership (Alexander VI) and secular leadership (Cesare Borgia). In 1513, the Medicis were similarly established: Pope Leo X (religious leader) and Lorenzo de Medici (secular leader). The author is showing the possibilities for this unique relationship in uniting Italy.

Finally, good leaders adapt to new circumstances, breaking old alliances and forming new ones when necessary. The overall message of the book is the promotion of analysis and adaptability in rulers. Such a message might be a statement of Machiavelli's willingness to adapt to the new leaders and serve them as well as he had served the Republic of Florence.

While many scholars agree that Machiavelli wrote *The Prince* to guide the Medicis and re-establish his favor, several see the treatise as satirical, or even as "bad advice offered as good advice" in hopes of unraveling the Medici regime. This was a widely held belief during the Enlightenment, and in Rousseau's seminal *The Social Contract*, Rousseau asserts, "Machiavelli was a proper man and a good citizen; but, being attached to the court of the Medici, he could not help veiling his love of liberty in the midst of his country's oppression. The choice of his detestable hero, Caesar Borgia, clearly enough shows his hidden aim; and the contradiction between the teaching of the Prince and that of the Discourses on Livy and the History of Florence shows that this profound political thinker has so far been studied only by superficial or corrupt readers. The Court of Rome sternly prohibited his book. I can well believe it; for it is that Court it most clearly portrays."

Rousseau

There are several reasons for this interpretation, some stemming from the text itself and some stemming from Machiavelli's biography. Obviously, Machiavelli had reason to hate the Medicis, so it seems counterintuitive that he would write a text instructing them how to establish stable rule, especially when he would be a danger to that rule and need to be eliminated. Although the book was dedicated to the Medicis, it was written in the vernacular—anomalous to most classical political and philosophical treatises. Some see this as an indication that the book was intended for the general public. This would make the text an expose of the leaders' immorality and, perhaps, an attempt to incite rebellion amongst the citizens.

Additionally, as Rousseau alluded to, *The Prince* contradicts Machiavelli's earlier political tracts, such as *The Discourses of Livy*, which praises republics over principalities. In fact, Machiavelli writes that the acts of princes "are cruel and destructive of all civilized life, and neither Christian, nor even human, and should be avoided by every one" (I.26). Some suggest that reading Machiavelli's oeuvre points to the absurdity of *The Prince* and its messages.

The text itself may point to this reading as well. For example, Machiavelli suggests that a good prince will arm his subjects. While he rationalizes this by claiming such an action will foster trust and goodwill between the prince and his subjects, it also creates a higher potential for a rebellion. Others suggest that Machiavelli's suggestion that the Medicis live in Florence will also make rebellion easier, especially if the republicans are armed.

The Prince derides principalities granted by fortune or gifting. The best princes gain their lands by martial prowess and the assent of the people. The Medicis regained Florence as a papal gift, and they had to quell the republicans. (According to Chapter Seven, such princes "stand simply upon the goodwill and the fortune of him who has elevated them—two most inconstant and unstable things" [1].) The Medicis also had to rely on auxiliary soldiers (Spanish troops) to do so, another bad choice for good princes. The example of Louis and the Switzers may be a warning of the Medici's weakened reputations.

For further reading on this topic, see Book III of Rousseau's *The Social Contract*, Mary Deitz's "Trapping the Prince," and Ian Johnston's *Lecture on Machiavelli's* The Prince.

Legacy of *The Prince*

It would be easier to enumerate the areas of the humanities and social sciences that have not been affected by Machiavelli's text, rather than those that have. The book is still widely reprinted and read in history, political science, literature, ethics, sociology, rhetoric, and religion classes, to name just a few. And the term "Machiavellian" has made its way into popular culture, although just how "Machiavellian" Machiavelli actually was is still up for debate.

The Prince was significant in shifting humanist ideals towards a more secular view of human affairs. Rather than looking to God for answers and explanations for answers about human interactions, Machiavelli's text suggests that analysis of rulers and their power struggles could answer many previously unexplained occurrences. And whether or not any aspect or result of the Protestant Reformation can be attributed to *The Prince*, the humanist ideals were certainly significant in the distrust of mediators in religious matters. Thomas Cromwell and England's Henry VIII both read the text and commented that it influenced their shift towards Protestantism (although the shift was much more complex than a simple application of any one book).

Henry VIII

Machiavelli was no less influential on Enlightenment thought of the seventeenth and eighteenth centuries. Rene Descartes and other materialist philosophers found Machiavelli's emphasis on rationality and man's control over his own existence especially helpful in enunciating their own beliefs.

Moral philosophers also frequently credit *The Prince* as being one of the cornerstones of their thoughts. Machiavelli's promotion of relative morality was influential on philosophers such as David Hume and Adam Smith. The idea that moral action is contingent upon location and time still pervades modern thought in poststructuralist and anthropological principles.

Hume

Machiavelli is also known as the father of modern political science. Before *The Prince*, most politicians relied on classical philosophers such as Plato and Aristotle for guidance on politics. But Machiavelli's pragmatic approach to politics, using empirical observation, replaced the classical idealistic concepts. Enlightenment thinkers such as David Hume, John Locke, and even Thomas Jefferson drew heavily from the methodology set forth in *The Prince*.

Made in the USA
Las Vegas, NV
18 October 2021